Carnataurus

The Horned Predator

Dinosaur Books For Young Readers
By
Enrique Fiesta

Mendon Cottage Books

JD-Biz Publishing

I0440135

Read More Amazing Animal Books

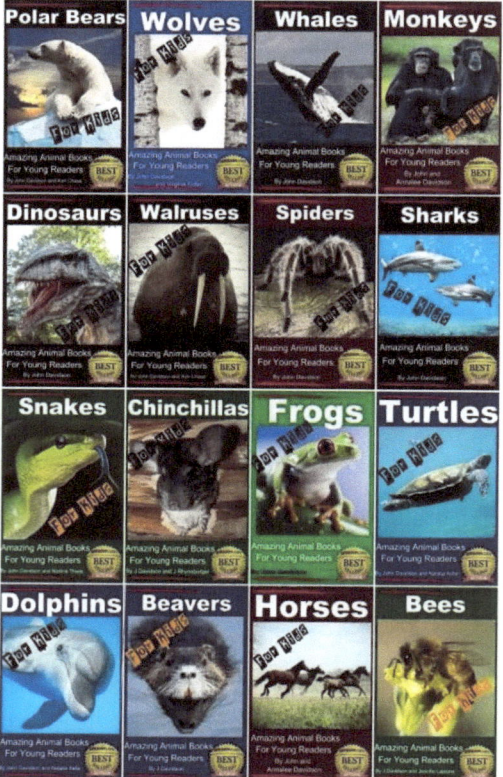

Purchase at Amazon.com

Table of Contents

Introduction

We are going to go on a journey back to the age of the dinosaurs to check out one of the strangest dinosaurs to ever have existed. That dinosaur is the Carnotaurus. The Carnotaurus is called a Carnotaur for short. The Carnotaurus was a strange creature because of the peculiar horns which grew from the top of its head and because of the many distinct characteristics is possesses that other similar dinosaurs did not have. For instance the Carnotaur was a lightly built predator whereas the t-rex was a large, bulking and heavy set predator even though both predators have tiny arms and walked on two legs.

We are going to check out the reasons why the Carnotaur had the horns it had and we are going to check out all of its other nifty characteristics. It should be noted though that to appreciate dinosaurs properly, it takes more than just fossils and facts. One really has to have genuine wonder and interest in what the dinosaurs were- and this takes a bit of imagination. One really needs to understand that the dinosaurs were amazing creatures which came in all shapes and sizes and which really probably never exist again. That means we have to make images in our mind about how the dinosaurs looked, how they acted, and even how they smelled and what they sounded like. When you really imagine what the dinosaurs were you start to experience wonder and awe about just how mysterious and cool nature and earth really are. Now let's take a step back in time and walk with the dinosaurs!

Chapter 1: Appearance

The Carnotaur was a peculiar predator because of the way it was built and what it looked like. The Carnotaur was what paleontologists (scientists who study dinosaurs) called a predatory therapod. A predator is a dinosaur which eats meat; we will talk about the Carnotaur's predatory behavior in the next chapter. What is important to note is that most of the well-known predatory therapods like the Tyrannosaurus Rex, the Spinosaurus, and the Gigantosaurus were large, bulky, and very heavy. The Tyrannosaur weighed about 9 tons! Unlike these predatory therapods the Carnotaur was lightly built and would have looked quite slim if it was standing next to the Tyrannosaur. The Carnotaur could reach a height of about 10 feet and a length of about 30 feet and it weighed almost two tons. That means that the Carnotaur is about four feet taller than the average human and more than ten times the weight! The Carnotaur was also an incredibly muscular dinosaur. The tail of this dinosaur was held straight and did not drag on the ground, and it too was muscled. Paleontologists can determine how muscled a dinosaur was based on its fossil remains. Fossils are the remains of ancient animals and other organisms- and they are clues which help scientists make guesses about what the dinosaurs looked like and how they behaved. For instance, the fossils of the Carnotaur possess no feather-knobs (areas where feathers attach to bone) which tells us that the Carnotaur was not covered in feathers like some other dinosaurs, but that it was covered in scales.

We do not know what color the scales of the Carnotaur were, but we can use our imaginations and make educated guesses by looking at the dinosaurs that are still alive. For instance, the Carnotaur could have been green, brown, or tan in order to blend in with its environment. Lions, alligators, and most predators are the color of their environment which is what helps them catch prey unawares. They may have even changed colors like a chameleon- chameleons are predators, have horns, and also have scales- just like a Carnotaur! It may even have been brightly colored like some birds are today; the red cardinal does not blend in with its surroundings and it is a predator. The possibilities are almost endless!

The size of this dinosaur greatly exceeds the size of a human but what makes the Carnotaur particularly frightening is its deadly array of teeth. The Carnotaurus possessed a mouth full of long and slender teeth and paleontologists believe that the Carnotaur possessed a bite-force more than twice the strength of an American Alligator's. The American Alligator has a bite-force of almost 3,000 pounds! That is enough force to lift most cars off of the ground. Imagine what a Carnotaur could do with its teeth!

The most distinguishing mark of the Carnotaur, other than its large size yet small build, is the pair of horns which protrude from the top of the dinosaur's eyebrows. This is a peculiar characteristic which no other predatory dinosaur possesses and scientists are baffled as to what they were used for. We will talk about some of those theories in the next chapter. Here is a fun fact: the Carnotaur actually received its name because of its horns. The name "Carnotaurus" is actually two words combined- the Latin words *carnis* (flesh) and *taurus* (bull) fuse together to make "Carnotaurus" which literally means "flesh-eating bull." If you are going to study dinosaurs, it is a really good idea to learn some Latin and Ancient Greek.

The Carnotaur had another characteristic which makes it different from its distant relatives: the Carnotaur had the shortest arms of them all! The Carnotaur's arms were heavily muscled and this baffles scientists because they do not know what a Carnotaur could have done with such tiny, muscular arms.

Chapter 2: Behavior

The Carnotaur was a predator which means that it hunted and ate other animals. The evidence for this are the long, slender teeth and large size of this dinosaur. Scientists do not know exactly how the Carnotaur hunted or exactly what it ate. Some scientists believe that the Carnotaur only ate small creatures; creatures the size of humans or large dogs. They believe that the Carnotaur would stab its prey with its teeth and trap them because the shape of the teeth were slanted in such a way that the prey could not escape.

Other scientists believe that the Carnotaur was able to bring down large prey- even sauropods. Sauropods is the scientific name for those large, quadrupedal (walked on four legs), long-necked, herbivorous (plant-eating) dinosaurs. They point out that the Carnotaur possesses a build and frame which could support powerful, strong muscles and that it was lightly-built. A lightly-built and strong predator is what we call in layman's terms a "lean, mean, killing machine." If the Carnotaur possessed the muscle power and speed indicated by its fossils then it would have been one of the fastest dinosaurs ever to have existed. This means that it would have been the cheetah of the dinosaur age.

It is unknown as to what the horns on the Carnotaur's head were used for. They are solid bone and triangular in shape. Some scientists believe the Carnotaur used them when hunting; the Carnotaur would head-butt his prey with the horns in order to deliver serious injuries to the prey. Other scientists believe they were for display- like modern day rams and deer. The more prominent the horns the more likely the Carnotaur would be able to attract a mate. Neither theory can be proven for sure yet, but it is still fun to sit and think about it.

Unfortunately, only one Carnotaur fossil has been found intact which means that there is limited information available for scientists to work with. Besides the Carnotaur being a predator, most of its behavior is open to interpretation. For instance, it is possible that the Carnotaur was a pack predator. A pack predator is a predatory animal which hunts socially, a member of a group. Some cartoons and television shows have depicted the Carnotaur in this way. This is not an unfounded speculation, as many predators today hunt in groups and there is evidence that other therapods hunted in groups (raptors for instance). Unfortunately, there is not enough information to say anything binding at this time.

Chapter 3: Where and When

The Carnotaur lived in the plains of South America during the Late Cretaceous Period. This period was the last period of the dinosaur age (Triassic, Jurassic, and Cretaceous). At the end of the Late Cretaceous Period the dinosaurs perished during the Dinosaur Extinction Event. What occurred during the Extinction Event is unknown- disease, climate change, or a meteoric impact.

The plains ranged from estuaries, tidal flats, and coastlands. This means that the Carnotaur would have lived near water during its lifetime. The Carnotaur lived with a range of other dinosaurs with which it either hunted, lived peacefully, or competed with. Remember it is difficult to determine what dinosaurs it lived with because only one fossil has been found. It could have lived with Gigantosaurus, Rinconosaurus, Abelisaurus, and Pterodon.

The Gigantosaurus was a large therapod, even larger than Tyrannosaurus, and was most likely the apex predator of the South American. It was large and stronger than the Carnotaur and would probably hunt a Carnotaur if the occasion called for it. The Carnotaur, though, was much faster and could probably have escaped a Gigantosaurus if necessary. This relationship could be paralleled with that of lions to cheetahs; lions hunt and kill cheetahs because lions are larger but cheetahs are faster.

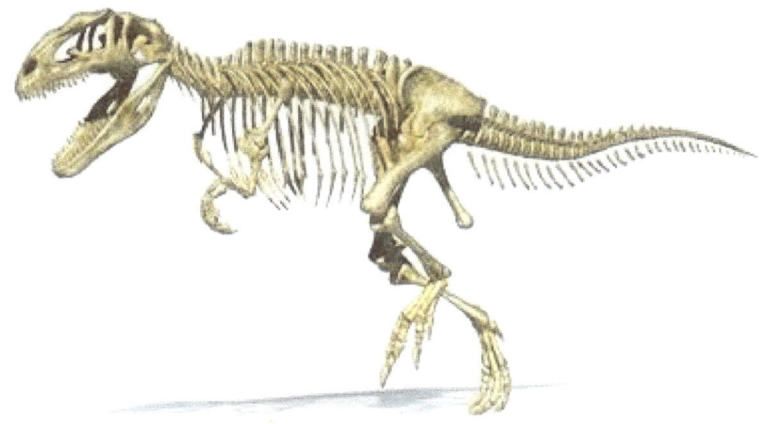

The Rinconosaurus was a long-necked dinosaur (sauropod) and could have been a potential food source and prey for the Carnotaur. The Carnotaur would most likely have quickly sprinted toward the dinosaur and either head-butt the sauropod with his bony horns or just chomped down on the neck of the sauropod with this teeth.

The Abelisaurus was another dinosaur of approximately the same size. The Abelisaurus was also a predatory therapod, but unlike the Gigantosaurus was probably unable to kill a Carnotaur easily. The two dinosaurs would have competed for prey but would have most likely avoided directly attacking one another (unless of course one of these dinosaurs was a pack hunter; then the pack could take down members of opposing species with ease).

The Pterodon was an ancient flying dinosaur, This dinosaur probably did not compete with the Carnotaur and the Carnotaur most likely did not hunt it. The Pterodon was primarily a fish-eating dinosaur. It would have soared in the skies above the Carnotaur.

Conclusion

The environment of the Carnotaur was lush and went through dry and humid seasons. We have stepped back in time to look at this dinosaur, where and when he lived, the dinosaurs he lived with, and what a journey it was! By using our imaginations and knowledge we can engage, wonder about, and appreciate the wonderful mystery of the dinosaurs. By learning about and appreciating what the dinosaurs were we come to appreciate our own present age and all the wonderful creatures that live today. We discover how varied and mysterious life really is- we look at animals today with special reverence and awe because one day they might not ever exist; just like the dinosaurs. Make sure you keep thinking, keep learning, and keep imagining.

Author Bio

Enrique Fiesta

I was born in Southwest Florida and I hold a degree in Latin and Greek language and literature. In addition to my principal studies, I have also studied philosophy, history, the natural sciences, and literature. In my spare time I devote the vast majority of my time to reading, writing, praying, and walking. I am currently pursuing legal studies in order to become an attorney.

Our books are available at
1. Amazon.com
2. Barnes and Noble
3. Itunes
4. Kobo
5. Smashwords
6. Google Play Books

Bonus Dinosaur Content

Introduction to Dinosaurs

We will start our journey with dinosaurs with the Tyrannosaurus Rex. The fossilized remains of the Tyrannosaurus are found in the world's biggest dig sites, which are located in Montana. Palaeontologists discover new things about dinosaurs in dig sites. Dinosaurs can be huge, weird, tiny and even wonderful. The Tyrannosaurus Rex, as we will find out, was one of the huge dinosaurs palaeontologists have discovered.

Tyrannosaurus Rex

The word dinosaur is derived from the ancient Greek words "deinos" and "saurus." These words translated into English mean "terrible lizard." Dinosaurs were creatures who dwelled on Earth and dominated the life of this planet during the Mesozoic Era which was about 65 million years ago. There were also flying and marine dinosaurs and they existed with the land-dwelling dinosaurs for about 150 million years. Dinosaurs occupied every kind of environment and climate which existed on Earth at those times. They could be about as small as the size of chicken to being 100 feet long and weighing 100 tons. Dinosaurs were one of two types: one was called Ornithischia which means bird hipped, and the other Saurischia which means lizard hipped. Dinosaurs could either be herbivorous, carnivorous or omnivorous. These are long extinct animals- there are no more dinosaurs today.

Microraptor© *Michael Rosskothen - Fotolia.com*

Facts about Dinosaurs

Have you ever heard of Dinosaurs? What are they? Here are some important facts about them.

1. Dinosaurs are reptiles that lived on earth over 230 million years ago.

2. The word Dinosaur originated from Greek words "terrible lizard."

3. Dinosaurs are extinct and cannot be found on earth alive right now, but their fossils can be extracted for study.

4. The heaviest dinosaurs weighed about 80 tons, and they are called brachiosaurs. Brachiosaurs had a height of 16 meters and a length of 26 meters.

5. Dinosaurs laid eggs which can be found in many shapes and sizes. The smallest egg of a dinosaur ever found on earth is about 3 centimeters in length and a large one was about 30cm in length.

6. When dinosaur eggs become fossils they harden like rocks but maintain their structure.

7. Troodon was probably the most intelligent dinosaur. Its cranial capacity was equal to that of an average present day mammal. It had grasping hands and stereoscopic vision.

8. Ornithomiminds were the fastest dinosaurs. They were able to reach maximum speeds of 60 kilometers per hour.

Fight between Euoplocephalus tutus and Troodon formosus

9. The oldest dinosaur bones are found in Madagascar and they are around 230 million years old.

10. Micropachycephalosaurus is the longest name of a dinosaur and it means tiny thick headed lizard .It was discovered in China.

11. Thecodontosaurus Antiquus was the oldest dinosaur to be discovered in Britain .It was discovered in 1970 in a place near Bristol. It was 2.1 meters in length.

12. Up to the present over 700 species of dinosaurs have been discovered and named. Palaeontologists are carrying out more research with the aim of discovering more.

13.108 species of dinosaurs have been discovered in Britain alone.

14. Megalosaurus was the first dinosaur to be formerly named. It was named in 1824.

Dinosaur Extinction

The term extinction is used in biology to refer to the end of a species. Dinosaurs became extinct 65 million years ago at the end of the Cretaceous period. Since this took place many years ago, it is hard for scientists to find the reason that caused the dinosaurs to become extinct. Rocks and fossils are used by scientists to find out what caused the dinosaur extinction. However, there are some plausible explanations for what could have happened.

The explanations put forward include:

Volcanic eruptions
Volcanic eruption are one of the suggested reasons. According to this suggestion, there was a lot of volcanic activity that caused changes in the weather. The dinosaurs were not able to adapt to the weather changes and so they died.

Diseases
Diseases could also have caused the death of the dinosaurs. A disease could have spread rapidly and killed them.

The Ice age
The climate of the planet occasionally becomes colder. These cold-periods are called ice ages and they might have killed off the dinosaurs if they could not survive in the colder weather.

Asteroid impact

Scientists believe that a very big asteroid hit the earth during the age of the dinosaurs. An asteroid impact could have altered weather patterns and possibly lowered the temperature of the planet. This is because an asteroid impact would have ejected tons of dust particles into the sky which would have blocked sunlight. If the sun is blocked plants cannot survive, then herbivores cannot survive, and then carnivores cannot survive.

Combined reasons or Gradual extinction
It is possible that no one factor alone was responsible for the death of the dinosaurs, but possibly a combination of volcanic eruptions, asteroid collisions, and outbreak of disease.

Dinosaur Fossils

Dinosaurs are animals that existed thousands of years ago. They are of different sizes and colors. Some have wings and other appear in their own physical appearance. Dinosaur fossils have been found all over the world.

Dinosaur Fossil

Fossils are what is left of these great animals. The bones that they left behind have been turned into rock over time. Today scientists can study these great animals by finding the fossils they left behind.

Dinosaur Eggs

Dinosaur eggs have been found all over the world. Some of them are very similar to large ostrich eggs found today. They have been fossilized over time and that is why we can still find them today. They generally tend to have more symmetry and a rounder shape than modern bird eggs. Baby dinosaurs found in fossilized eggs can be studied to learn more about the nature of these wonderful animals.

Dinosaur Egg

Dinosaur Names

The following are common dinosaur names and their meanings. Most names are coined from Greek vocabulary, but some dinosaurs are named after their place where they were discovered.

1. Albertosaurus -"Lizard of Alberta" refers to the fact that it was discovered in
Alberta.

2. Allosaurus -"Strange Lizard" due to its unusual bone structures.

3. Apatosaurus-"Deceptive Lizard" because it had bones similar to another dinosaur's bones. The confusion caused by this fact made the discoverer call the dinosaur deceptive.

4. Baryonyx -"Heavy Claw" because the first fossil to be found was a claw, and because this dinosaur's hands have large claws.

5. Brontosaurus- "Thunder Beast"

6. Coelophysis -"Hollow form"

7. Cynognathus -"Dog jawed" , because it has a jaw like a dog.

8. Deinonychus -"Terrible claw", refers to the large claws on its feet.

9. Dilophosaurus -"Two-crested lizard" because of the protuberances on its head.

10. Dimetrodon -"Two size of teeth" because it has a set of large teeth and a set of small teeth.

11. Dimorphodon- "Two types of teeth" possessed two different types of teeth, which is noteworthy for a reptile.

12. Diplocaulus- "Double stalk."

13. Diplodocus -"Double beamed lizard."

14. Dolichorhynchops -"Long-nosed snout."

15. Dromaesaurus -"Running lizard."

16. Elasmosaurus -"Thin plated lizard."

17. Gallimimus -"Bird mimic" because this dinosaur looks like a bird.

18. Giganotosaurus-"Giant lizard of south" refers to the gigantic size of this dinosaur.

19. Hesperonis- "Regal western bird."

20. Ichthyosaurus -"Fish lizard" because this dinosaur lived in the ocean.

21. Iguanodon -"Iguana tooth" the tooth of this dinosaur resembled that of an iguana.

22. Kronosaurus- "Titan lizard" refers to this dinosaur's large size.

23. Liopleurodon -"Smooth-sided teeth."

24. Maiasaurus -"Good mother lizard."

25. Megalodon -"Big-toothed shark" because this shark has enormous teeth.

26. Mosasaurus- "Meuse lizard."

27. Nothosaurus - "False lizard."

28. Ornitholestes-"Bird robber."

29. Ornithomimus-"Bird mimic" because of its bird-like appearance.

30. Oviraptor- "Egg thief" because they were believed to be taking eggs of other animals.

31. Plesiosaurs -"Close to lizard."

32. Pliosaurs -"More lizards."

33. Protoceratops-"First horn face" because of its single horn.

34. Pteradactyl- "Winged-fingered lizard" because of its long fingers which seemed to form a wing.

35. Pteranodon -"Winged, without teeth" because this dinosaur has a toothless beak and wings.

36. Quetzacoatlus- was named after the Aztec god Quetzalcoatl.

37. Saltopus -"Jumping Foot", because the first fossil found of this dinosaur was a leaping foot.

38. Spinosaurus- "Thorn lizard" because of the paddle-like spines protruding from its back.

39. Stegosaurus- "Roofed lizard" because it had bones on the back.

40. Suchomimus -"Crocodile mimic" because it looks like a crocodile in appearance.

41. Triceratops -"Three-horned face" refers to the three horns protruding from this dinosaurs head.

42. Trilobites- "Three lobes" refers to the tripartite structure of this creature's body.

43. Troodon- "Wounding tooth" refers to the dinosaur's sharp teeth.

44. Tyrannosaurus Rex -"Tyrant lizard" because this dinosaur is terrible to behold.

45. Utahraptor- "Robber from Utah", this dinosaur was named after the
place it was first discovered.

46. Velociraptor- "Speedy robber."

47. Yangchuanosaurus -"Yanchuan Lizard" because it was discovered in Yangchua.

Dinosaur Diet

The diet of an average dinosaur consisted either of plants, meat, insects, or some combination of the above. The dinosaurs which ate plants exclusively are called herbivores which literally means "plant eater." These dinosaurs ate fruit, leaves, grass, and roots from the earth and from trees. These dinosaurs possessed blunt, interlocking teeth which allowed them to easily grind up their vegetable diet. Some of these dinosaurs would eat rocks to help them digest their meals. It is speculated that these dinosaurs ate a lot, drank a lot, and slept a lot.

Other dinosaurs were carnivores which literally means "meat eater." These dinosaurs are more famous than herbivores because they are commonly depicted as the antagonists in dinosaur movies: think Tyrannosaurus Rex. Carnivores would hunt other dinosaurs down and eat them in order to feet. If they were anything like modern day predators, their primary source of food was herbivorous dinosaurs.

Carnivores were built for speed and possessed sharp teeth and sharp talons. They would use their speed to catch their prey, their claws to grip the grey, and their teeth to kill their prey. Some of these predators lived in packs and they would hunt together in order to bring down large prey they would otherwise not be able to kill.

Omnivores were dinosaurs which ate meat, insects, and vegetation. Omnivore literally means "all-eater." These dinosaurs would generally eat whatever was commonly available and sometimes they were scavengers. Scavengers eat the remains of animals which were killed by carnivores. These dinosaurs were specially adapted because they could survive in environments where other dinosaurs would die. If an area lacked meat or vegetation, an omnivore would survive but a herbivore or carnivore would die because of lack of food.

Feathered Dinosaurs

Shandong Tianyu Museum's discovery of partial pieces of fossils suggest that certain dinosaurs had feathers. A small skeleton of a dinosaur discovered later proved that the museum was correct. The fossil possessed feathers. Now scientists are speculating that a large variety of dinosaurs possessed feathers and these discoveries back up scientist's claims that some dinosaurs evolved into modern-day birds. Many of these feathered fossils are being discovered in China. These feathered dinosaurs possessed very complex and unique teeth. They were pointed, sharp, and peculiarly large. The teeth in their back jaws were broad and flat. Their teeth seem to indicate that they were able to eat both meat and vegetation, thus making them omnivores.

Plant Eating Dinosaurs

Herbivorous dinosaurs were well adapted to eating plants because of their teeth and long neck. Their teeth were built specially for grinding down plant matter, and some dinosaurs had long necks which allowed them to eat from the tops of trees. The following dinosaurs are common herbivorous dinosaurs.

1. Sauropodomorphs
They are also known as prosauropods. They consist of dinosaurs such as Plateosaurus ,Massopondylus, Lufengosaurus and Anchisaurus. They were able to feed on trees up to a height of 1.2 meters. They had well adapted teeth which were roughened and diamond shaped which allowed for easy tearing of vegetation. They had thick muscles at the gizzards that helped to break down the food.

2. Ornithischains
They had horny peak that was sharp and protruding out of the mouth for cropping plants. Teeth were adapted for tearing the picked plant food before swallowing. They had a fleshy cheek which covered parts of the side of their mouths. In this group there were dinosaurs such as lesothosaurus, Orodromes and the Scelosaurus.

3. Larger ornithopods
They included dinosaurs such as Ouranosaurus, Iguanodonand, Hadrosaurus. They had a beak which was sharp and broad for picking plant foods. They had interlocking teeth which allowed them to tear vegetation easily.

4. Larger ceratopians

They had extremely narrow beak which resembles that of a parrot. The beak was used to feed on vegetation by cutting the vegetation. They had more than one hundred teeth behind the beak; the teeth were interlocking for easy chewing of the plants picked. Psittacosaurus was a ceratopian.

The Weirdest Dinosaurs

Let's discuss a few of the weirdest dinosaurs known to humans.

Oviraptor- This dinosaur looked very similar to a modern day ostrich.
Oviraptor was weird in the sense that it already had bird like features before it became extinct.

Ouranosaurs- They had spines coming out of their backbone which means it had a sail on its back, or a large hump of flesh like a modern day camel. Since it was discovered in a desert, it is possible that it was a camel-like dinosaur.

Carnotaurus- Looked like a tiny Tyrannosaurs Rex. The Carnotaur had horns on its eyebrows and incredibly tiny arms.

Mamenchisaurus was herbivore but what made it weird was the length of its neck. It had an enormous 35-40 foot neck and not
surprisingly, it could never stretch it to full length upwards but had to carry it parallel to the ground.

The Deadliest Dinosaurs

Here are some of the deadliest dinosaurs. These dinosaurs were the lions, tigers, and bears of their time, only much, much larger.

1.Tyrannosaurus Rex
It had numerous strong and sharp teeth. This dinosaur was incredibly large and was probably the apex predator wherever it lived.

2. Utahraptor dinosaur
It had single curved claws which looked like a knife attached to its feet. These dinosaurs might have hunted in packs which made bringing down prey an easier task.

3 Jeholopterus
This dinosaur had sharp fangs. It is believed that the Jeholopterus made a living by sucking blood from other dinosaurs such as large sauropods (long-neck dinosaurs).

4. Kronosaurus
This is believed to have been bigger than the present great white shark. It possessed bigger teeth and a bigger jaw size. Think of a whale-sized shark coming after you.

5. Allosaurus
The Allosaurus was a fierce predator. This is proven by its very powerful jaws and sharp claws.

6. Sarcosuchus

This was the largest crocodile of the dinosaur age. Its length was double that of the largest crocodiles today and its weight was equal to 10 modern-day crocodiles. It had a long and powerful neck which allowed it to jump out of the water with lightning-quick speed.

7. Giganotosaurus

It had a weight of about 8 tons and three strong fingers on each of its hands. It was the largest predator that ever existed on earth. A full grown Gigantosaurus was probably able to bring down full-grown sauropods (long-neck dinosaurs).

Flying Dinosaurs

There are several species of dinosaurs which could fly or glide. Here are four of the flying dinosaurs that inhabited the earth millions of years ago.

Dimorphodon is one of the flying dinosaurs that existed during the age of reptiles. This type of dinosaur had two kinds of teeth and it was around 3.3 feet in length with a wing span of 4 feet. Due to its inability to stand and walk, this dinosaur spent a lot of time perched when not flying.

Dimorphodon

Rhamphorhynchus in another flying dinosaur that had short legs, a long tail that was made of ligaments, and a wing span of 3 feet in length. It had a narrow jaw with very sharp teeth and had a beak which it probably used to catch fish.

Rhamphorhynchus

The *Quetzalcoatlus* was discovered in North America and it is known to be one of the largest flying reptiles during the time dinosaurs were living on earth. Its wing span was 36 feet in length, and it had large eyes, a crested head, a very thin beak and its weight is speculated to have been around 300 pounds. The bones of this flying dinosaur were hollow which meant it could fly for very long distances.

Quetzalcoatlus

The *Pterodactyus* lived near water and its diet consisted of fish and other kinds of small animals. Its wing span was 20 to 30 inches.

Kinds of Dinosaurs

There were many different types of dinosaurs. Here is how scientists have classified them.

Dino Basics
A famous British scientist named Harry Seeley, in 1800's proposed a classification based on their hip structure. Seeley classified two major groups called Ornithischia (bird-hipped) and Saurischia (lizard-hipped). These two types were further broken down into sub groups as follows:

Ornithischia
Thyreophora: Also known as the armored dinosaurs, these dinosaurs were herbivores (plant eaters) and lived in the early Jurassic to the late Creaceous age. Thyrephora simply means "shield bearers" because these type of dinosaurs had armor, plates and horns. This group included Stegosaurus, Ankylosaurusand Nodosauus.

Ornithischia

Cerapods: These are typically horned or duck-billed dinosaurs Just like the Thyreophora, Cerapods were herbivores however, these dinosaurs has better teeth that helped them grind plants better. Cerapods were able to extract more nutrients from their food because of their more advanced jaws.

Saurischia
Theropods: The name means "beast feet." Typically, these dinosaurs moved on two legs and were carnivores (meat eaters). Some of these kinds of dinosaurs were also omnivores (ate both plants and meat). Theropods lived from the late Triassic period until the end of Cretaceous period. Scientists have also discovered that birds are the evolved-descendants of Theropods. While the scary looking and most popular ones in this category are the Tyrannosaurus Rex and Veliociraptor, there were also other dinosaurs like Spinosaurus, Deinonychus, Allosaurus, Carnotaurus,

Albertosaurus, Megalosaurus, Yangchuanosaurus and much more.

Sauropods: These lizard-footed type of dinosaurs walked on four legs and were enormous in size. They had long necks and tails, were huge in size and had comparatively small heads. Sauropods were herbivores and included Brachiosaurus, Diplodocus, Seismosaurus, Giraffatitan, and Apatosaurus.

The Biggest Dinosaurs

During the Jurassic period there were many heavy, gigantic dinosaurs that roamed all throughout the earth. Some of the biggest dinosaurs are listed below:

Liopleurodon - Liopleurodon looked similar to an orca and a shark, and it was the biggest pliosaur. It had a massive body, huge flippers, and a long thick jaw full of teeth. Palaeontologists say that this type of dinosaur weighed over 30 tons and could grow to a length of 50 feet.

Quetzalcoatlus - This type of dinosaur was also huge in size as it had a wingspan of 45 feet. This huge pterosaur has received its name from the winged Aztec god.

Spinosaurus - Spinosaurus was heavier than Tyrannosaurus Rex and it is believed that they were bigger in size too. It had a mouth that was similar to crocodile's mouth and it also had a skin flap that protruded from its back which resembled a sail. It is believed that the sail helped the dinosaur regulate its body temperature.

Argentinosaurus - As the name suggests, the fossils of this dinosaur was found in Argentina. It was among the biggest dinosaurs with weight of over 100 tons and height of up to 120 feet. A single spinal vertebra is four feet in diameter.

Argentinosaurus

The Smallest Dinosaurs

Fossils have helped palaeontologists discover the smallest dinosaurs that lived on earth. They are as follows: The Humming Bird - It may seem strange, but palaeontologists believe that dinosaurs did not become extinct completely but underwent evolution. Humming birds are believed to be the evolutionary descendants of dinosaurs that lived millions of years ago. It weighs as little as one-tenth of an ounce, and is considered to be the smallest dinosaur species that lives today.

Lariosaurus - With a total weight of about 20 pounds and a length of 2 feet, this dinosaur was the smallest aquatic dinosaur. It had a long pointed tail and a streamlined body. It usually lived in water but it also dwelt on land. It was similar to amphibians because it could live in both environments.

Pterosaurus - Pterosaurus had hollow bones and were lightly built. The pterosaurs were of different sizes but the smallest one was just a few inches long. This carnivorous dinosaur ate insects, crabs and fishes.

Microceratops - The microceratops was the smallest herbivorous dinosaur. It weighed 4 pounds and had a height of about a foot and a half.

Microaptor - The microaptors were the smallest carnivorous dinosaurs. They had a height of just 2 feet from head to tail. They were also known as "four-winged dinosaur" because they had feathers on their legs and arms. Their diet consisted only of insects.

Author Bio

Enrique Fiesta

I was born in Southwest Florida and I hold a degree in Latin and Greek language and literature. In addition to my principal studies, I have also studied philosophy, history, the natural sciences, and literature. In my spare time I devote the vast majority of my time to reading, writing, praying, and walking. I am currently pursuing legal studies in order to become an attorney. After I earn my law degree I intend to pursue a doctorate in philosophy, literature, and politics.

Our books are available at
1. Amazon.com
2. Barnes and Noble
3. Itunes
4. Kobo
5. Smashwords
6. Google Play Books

Publisher

JD-Biz Corp

P O Box 374

Mendon, Utah 84325

http://www.jd-biz.com/

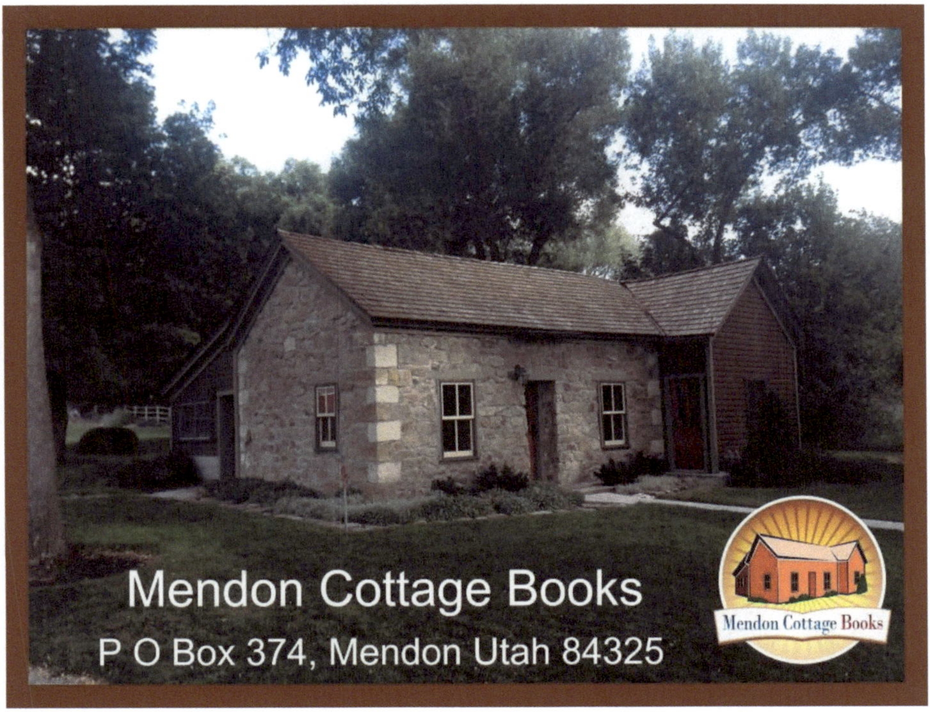

Mendon Cottage Books

P O Box 374, Mendon Utah 84325

Top Ten Dog Breeds For Kids

Amazing Animal Books
For Young Readers
Kisha Bennett & John Davidson

Poodles

Dog Books for Kids
K. Bennett

Labrador Retrievers

Dog Books for Kids
K. Bennett

German Shepherds

Dog Books for Kids
K. Bennett

Rottweilers

Dog Books for Kids
K. Bennett

Boxers

Dog Books for Kids
K. Bennett

Golden Retrievers

Dog Books for Kids
K. Bennett

Beagles

Dog Books for Kids
K. Bennett

Yorkies

Dog Books for Kids
K. Bennett

www.ingramcontent.com/pod-product-compliance
Lightning Source LLC
Chambersburg PA
CBHW050821290526
45792CB00001B/213